PRODUCE
— AND —
PROSPER

Transform Your Productivity With Proven Skills
and Mindsets for Unprecedented Success

ABRAHAM O. OWOSENI, Ph.D.

I see him as a master life designer; he has influenced thousands of lives the world over through his speaking engagements, books, and most importantly, his life.
David Igbokwe

I can best describe him as someone who impacts lives with the entirety of his being.
Omotola Olori

He is someone who obviously knows his onions and is confident in what the "Manufacturer" has called him to do – and the fruits are obvious!
Tola Adefidipe

Abraham is one of the most passionate speakers I have ever met; his passion for youth empowerment is exceptional. He is the pure example of the kind of leaders and change-makers the world needs.
Daniel Ojinaka

His inspiring words can never go stale. He continues to release truth and words of wisdom for the current and future generations.
Damilola Eluyela

He has a unique way of teaching that will never leave you the same.
Emmanuel Adeifa

One of the most eloquent and passionate speakers and mentors I ever met.
Sonia Jerry-Okondu

Abraham O. Owoseni

CONTENTS

Foreword	7
Introduction	10
Just Before We Begin	13
The Gauge of Productivity	16

    Explore the foundational principles of productivity and learn how to enhance your productivity levels.

The Blueprint of Productivity	28

    Discover how to transform your God-given gifts into purposeful products, for maximum impact and fulfilment.

Reproducing and Multiplying	43

    Learn how to expand your personal effectiveness and achieve greater success by scaling productive practices

Personal Productivity and National Productivity —The Ripple Effect   56

    Understand how personal productivity contributes to national economic success.

The Production Process: A Seven-Step Guide	62

    Follow a structured seven-step approach to design, implement, and refine effective production processes

The Remarkable Productivity of Joseph and Daniel	93

    Explore the exceptional productivity of Joseph and Daniel, two biblical figures renowned for their innovation.

The Productivity Tree	109
End Notes	
Useful Resources	
Acknowledgements	
Transformed Lives	
About the Author	

Dedication

This book is dedicated to the army of productive giants God is raising across nations and territories. To those who will take up the mantle to fulfil God's mandate to reproduce and multiply: This is for you.

Foreword

Amidst the ceaseless cacophony of the global economy pegged on output and performance, Abraham Owoseni's *'Produce and Prosper'* could not have come at a better time. This book transcends mere motivational tips for working harder; it serves as a life-changing guide that translates divine calling into everyday practices in the contemporary world.

Dr. Abraham brings together biblical principles, scientific insights, and pragmatic approaches to reinvent the concept of productivity. He draws us back to the original command given to humanity: "Be fruitful and increase in number; fill the earth and subdue it." Through this lens, he encourages readers to view their occupations not merely as deliverables but as noble missions on earth.

A unique beneficial approach here is that the author takes a rather integrative view of people. Rather than simply teaching time management or motivational strategies, Abraham goes into the fundamentals of productivity by exploring how the gifts that God has provided can be transformed into tangible goods and services for the benefit of others.

Dr. Abraham Owoseni recognizes that efficiency is not confined to a profession or field of work, as is often perceived. Whether one operates in a professional, vocational, or entrepreneurial environment, this book offers valuable insights on enhancing performance.

Among the most useful sections is the seven-step guide to the process of "producing." It provides a systematic framework for transforming thoughts into tangible results, regardless of discipline. This section alone justifies the price of the book, offering practical guidance for changing your mindset and approach to innovation and creativity.

What I found particularly interesting about Abraham's presentation is his effort to draw a correlation between individual and national productivity. In essence, he conveys a clear notion that despite the intensity, the grand work is a cumulative effort of every worker where everyone's input counts in building a particular economy.

The stories of Joseph and Daniel exemplify how productivity translates into power and impact within organizational and national contexts. These biblical narratives are seamlessly integrated into modern business environments with principles, providing a formula for success.

As a productivity expert, I wholeheartedly support Owoseni's emphasis on spirituality in productivity. He reminds us that effectiveness is not solely about working harder but working smarter, and performing with intent and integrity.

'Produce and Prosper' is more than just a book; it is a call to action. It challenges readers to transform busyness into meaningful productivity in every sense of the word. Whether you are a seasoned professional seeking refinement or a young person entering the workforce, you will find this book filled with helpful tips and strategies to maximize your goals and achieve beyond your expectations.

In today's world, where many are on an endless quest for purpose in their careers, Owoseni provides a roadmap for achieving that purpose. This book is not just a guide to productivity; it is a guide on how you—yes, you—can create significant and lasting change in your sphere of influence and beyond.

Remi Dairo
President, Institute of Productivity and Business Innovation Management (IPBIM)
Fellow, World Academy of Productivity Science
CEO, Productivate Plus, Texas, United States

September 2024

Introduction

Productivity is more than a buzzword in corporate corridors or a metric on performance reviews. It's a fundamental aspect of our existence, deeply rooted in our purpose as human beings. In the beginning, when God created the heavens and the earth, He didn't just set the world in motion and step back. Instead, He issued a profound mandate to humanity, one that would shape our purpose and drive our actions for millennia to come: "God blessed them: 'Prosper! Reproduce! Fill Earth! Take charge! Be responsible for fish in the sea and birds in the air, for every living thing that moves on the face of Earth.'"[1]

These words, spoken at the dawn of creation, carry a weight and significance that resonates through the ages. They are not just a command, but a blessing—a divine endorsement of human productivity and stewardship. In this simple yet powerful statement, we find the blueprint for a life of purpose, impact, and unprecedented success.

But what does it mean to truly "produce and prosper" in today's world? In an age where busyness is often mistaken for productivity, where digital distractions compete fiercely for our attention, and where the lines between work and life are increasingly blurred, how do we fulfil this God-given mandate? How do we ensure that our efforts are not just a flurry of activity, but a meaningful contribution to the world around us?

This book, "Produce and Prosper," is your guide to answering these questions and more. It's an invitation to rediscover the divine purpose behind your daily tasks, to realign your efforts with God's intentions for your life, and to unlock levels of productivity and success you may have never thought possible.

Throughout these pages, we'll embark on a journey that transcends traditional productivity advice. Leveraging the combination of science, biblical wisdom, life coaching and pragmatic pedagogy, we'll explore the true meaning of productivity, how to gauge and improve your productivity; the art of reproduction and multiplication and the intricate connection between personal productivity and national prosperity. Ultimately, I'll show you the 'production process' and how to master it for optimal results.

Whether you're in ministry, or an entrepreneur building a business, in a professional, or vocational career, or simply someone seeking to make the most of the talents God has given you, this book has something for you.

Remember, you are part of a new breed—an army of

productive giants that God is raising across nations and territories. You have been called to take up the mantle of responsibility, to fulfil God's mandate to reproduce and multiply. So, are you ready to answer the call? Are you prepared to align your productivity with divine purpose, to reach new heights of fruitfulness in every aspect of your life? If so, turn the page and let's begin this transformative journey together.

Welcome to "Produce and Prosper"—your guide to transforming your productivity with proven skills and mindsets for unprecedented success. May these pages inspire you to reach new heights of fruitfulness in every aspect of your life, for His glory and the advancement of humanity.

Abraham O. Owoseni, Ph.D.
September, 2024

Just Before We Begin

Productivity isn't an isolated concept; it's inherently linked to how you apply yourself in your work and how you manage your tasks and time. It's about the quality and quantity of work you produce, and it plays a crucial role in your career.

But here's the challenge, many people limit their understanding of careers to traditional office work, often associated with specific "collar" colours. For instance, "white-collar" jobs refer to office-based roles that typically require professional, managerial, or administrative skills and formal education. Examples include accountants, lawyers, and office managers. On the other hand, "blue-collar" roles involve skilled trades and hands-on work, such as electricians, plumbers, and construction workers.

Regardless of your collar colour, having the right orientation about work is fundamental to productivity. Without a clear understanding of your role and responsibilities, it's challenging to be productive. A solid grasp of what your work entails is essential for effective performance. As I often share in my career coaching and resources: "A career encompasses your lifelong work and can be likened to a wheeled vehicle that includes all types of work—whether professional, vocational, or entrepreneurial." Your career is not just a job; it's your life's work.

So, where do you fit in? In "The Career Work Model," I outline three major categories of work:

1. **Professional Career**: This model typically requires specialized education, training, or certifications. Careers in fields such as law, medicine, engineering, finance, or education are examples. Professional careers usually follow a structured path with defined roles and responsibilities.

2. **Vocational Career**: This model focuses on specific trades or skilled occupations that require hands-on training and expertise. Examples include careers in plumbing, electrical work, carpentry, or culinary arts. Vocational careers emphasize technical skills and often involve certifications or apprenticeships rather than traditional academic degrees.

3. **Entrepreneurial Career**: This model involves creating and managing your own business or ventures. Entrepreneurs are responsible for all aspects of their business, from conception to execution. This path requires innovation, risk-taking, and a strong drive to turn ideas into successful enterprises.

Now, you understand what I mean when I refer to careers or to work. Everyone is a career person!

Also, note that no career model is inherently superior to the others; the key is to identify where you thrive the most. Additionally, hybrid careers can emerge, combining elements from two or more of these models. For example, a doctor who runs their own private practice blends professional and entrepreneurial aspects, or a skilled tradesperson who also teaches their craft combines vocational and professional elements. Hybrid careers blend various elements to create a unique and fulfilling career journey tailored to individual strengths and aspirations.

With this understanding, let's proceed! Productivity is not isolated. The goal is to be productive in your work, your career!

The Gauge of Productivity

"I've been very busy..."

It's a phrase we hear often—sometimes as an excuse for incomplete tasks, missed timelines or tasks that aren't deemed a top priority. But what does "busyness" really mean? According to Oxford Languages, busyness is "the state or condition of having a great deal to do." Merriam-Webster adds a useful variant: "the state of having or being involved in many activities."

From these definitions, we can draw a few inferences:

1. **Busyness vs. Productivity**: Being busy doesn't necessarily equate to being productive. You can have a lot to do without achieving meaningful results. As Peter Drucker, a renowned management consultant, asserts, "Efficiency is doing things right; effectiveness is doing the right things."[2] This distinction emphasises that productivity is not just about being busy, but about achieving outcomes that matter.

2. **Activities vs. Results**: Involvement in many activities doesn't always lead to tangible outcomes. True productivity comes from turning activities into results. If it ends at activities only, that's busyness, it the activities end into results, that's 'product-activity.' So, are you genuinely productive or just busy?

Here's why: busyness is merely a flurry of activities, whereas true productivity integrates activities with tangible results. Take a software developer, for instance, who spends hours writing code, debugging programs, and collaborating with teams to build applications or software solutions. The evidence of their productivity is not just in the time spent coding (activities) but in the quality and functionality of the software they deliver (results).

The results here can be measured in terms of successful project completions, bug-free software releases, mobile apps, robust enterprise software, cloud services, user satisfaction metrics, and innovations introduced to streamline processes.

We'd always have several kinds of activities; and like Stephen Covey's Time Management Matrix, there are four typical quadrants to categorize every activity into: urgent and important, not urgent but important, urgent but not important, and neither urgent nor important.[3] Covey argues that effective productivity focuses on activities that are important but not necessarily urgent. This approach fosters meaningful progress and helps prevent burnout from constantly addressing only urgent issues.

Reflect on whether your efforts lead to real progress and outcomes.

Cal Newport's concept of the "Inverted Pyramid of Productivity" provides a compelling framework for rethinking how we approach our work. The basic idea is that high-performing individuals, teams, and organizations spend the majority of their time focused on "high-leverage" activities - the vital few tasks that generate the greatest impact. In contrast, many of us get bogged down in a seemingly endless sea of "low-leverage" busywork that, while necessary, doesn't move the needle in a meaningful way.[4]

It's easy to fall into the trap of constantly checking emails, responding to messages, attending back-to-back meetings, and getting pulled into minor operational fires. While these types of activities can't be entirely avoided, the most productive people learn to ruthlessly prioritize their time and energy. They relentlessly guard their attention, carefully selecting the mission-critical problems they'll tackle each day.

Imagine an actual physical pyramid - the wide base represents all the low-leverage tasks that consume most people's days, while the narrow top contains the high-impact activities. High performers flip this pyramid on its head, making the high-leverage work the foundation of their productivity. They may spend 80% of their time on the vital 20% of their responsibilities, rather than getting dragged down by the trivial many.

This intentional inversion takes discipline and focus, but the payoff can be transformative. Spending more time in the "deep work" mode - periods of uninterrupted, cognitively demanding labour. It's a powerful reminder that true productivity is not about doing more, but about doing the right things exceptionally well.

Legendary management thinker Peter Drucker had a clear view on what makes organizations truly effective. He made an important distinction between efficiency and effectiveness. Drucker argued that efficiency is just a basic requirement for survival—it's about doing things well and using resources wisely. However, effectiveness is what truly makes a difference. It's about focusing on doing the right things, not just doing things right.[5]

For example, a tech startup could be efficient having well-organized processes and using its resources effectively, but if it's not addressing a real market need or offering a compelling product, its efficiency won't lead to success. An effective startup, however, would focus on creating innovative solutions that meet customer needs, even if it means adjusting its processes. How about a restaurant whose operations are efficient, with streamlined workflows, tight inventory control, and an attentive wait staff. But if the food is mediocre and the ambiance is uninviting, all that efficiency counts for little. An effective restaurant, on the other hand, would prioritize delivering an exceptional dining experience - crafting a mouth-watering menu, curating an inviting atmosphere, and delighting customers at every turn.

Another example is a personal fitness routine. If you're given an efficient workout plan that requires the use of gym equipment and time, but if it doesn't address your specific fitness goals or interests, it won't be as impactful. An effective workout plan, on the other hand, focuses on what will help you achieve your personal health goals and keep you motivated. This is interesting. Here are a few more examples: An efficient online learning course might deliver content quickly and use streamlined tools for student interaction. However, an effective course ensures that students deeply understand the material and can apply it in real-world scenarios.

Think about event planning. An efficient event planner handles logistics smoothly, ensures timely deliveries, and sticks to the budget. But an effective event planner creates a memorable experience for attendees, meets the event's objectives, and aligns with the client's vision. We have all interfaced with customer service from different aspects of life whether banking, communication, etc. What was your observation? Typically, you see a play out of an efficient team that processes complaints and inquiries quickly, managing a high volume of cases with minimal wait times. Sometimes, the replies are rigid and not tailored to direct enquiries, without much helps. Yet, an effective team not only resolves issues swiftly but also addresses the root causes of customer problems, leading to greater overall satisfaction and improved loyalty.

Another example is project management. An efficient project manager follows the plan meticulously, ensures tasks are completed on time, and manages resources effectively. An effective project manager, however, ensures that the project's outcomes align with strategic goals, addresses stakeholder needs, and adapts the plan as necessary to achieve the best results.

In our personal lives, we often get caught up in being more efficient—automating tasks, organizing our schedules, and optimizing routines. But key questions to ask would be: Am I focusing on what truly matters? Am I prioritizing the right activities over simply being productive? This mindset can change how we approach our work, relationships, and daily lives. Instead of just doing things efficiently, Drucker advises to concentrate on doing the right things—prioritizing what will have the greatest impact and lead to meaningful results.

Now, you might be wondering why it's crucial to focus on increasing your productivity. Here's a compelling reason to consider: "To those who use well what they are given, even more will be given, and they will have an abundance. But from those who do nothing, even what they have will be taken away."[6] I paraphrased it this way, "Those who make the most of their talents and resources will see their productivity multiply and enjoy great abundance. However, those who do nothing with what they have will find even their small gains diminishing." I share more on this in the subsequent chapter.

So, what do you have? And as John Obidi, the personal development maestro, would ask, 'How are you utilizing your TEAM of resources—your time, energy, attention, and money?' These resources are freely given to you, but remember, to whom much is given, much is expected. "Use what you have, for what you have is plenty," he added. Productivity isn't just about staying busy; it's about making impactful use of what you're given. Those who wisely manage and invest their team of resources will not only retain them but will see them grow. On the flip side, those who do nothing with their resources risk losing even the little they have. Inaction can lead to stagnation and loss, whereas productivity ensures progress and expansion.

In the coming chapters, I will guide you through the process of maximizing what you have to create greater global value and produce impactful results. This is the essence of productivity. Remember, "For the more you use, the more you will have. But from those who do nothing, even what little they have will be taken away."[7] Gauging your productivity is not just about measuring how busy you are, but about assessing the value and impact of what you produce.

Abraham O. Owoseni

Highest Learning Points

Take a moment to jot down and highlight the key insights and lessons that resonated with you most in this chapter.

Most Pressing Action Points

Take a moment to note down the key decisions and actions you would take based on the insights gained from this chapter.

The Blueprint of Productivity

Productivity is a term we often toss around to measure our effectiveness and worth in our career journeys. Organisations use appraisal systems to gauge this and reward high achievers. But let's take a deeper look at productivity and broaden its scope. Ready?

The word "productivity" combines "produce" and "activities." As professionals, understanding this helps us assess our own productivity. Let's contextualise the word, 'produce.' What's produce like across professional, vocational and entrepreneurial careers? For example, we're conversant with agricultural produce. These are goods grown and harvested from farmlands. The likes of crops such as fruits, vegetables, grains, as well as livestock like meat, and eggs. As a noun, "produce" typically refers to agricultural or natural output. As a verb, it means the act of bringing forth or yielding something. "Then God said, 'Let the land produce vegetation: seed-bearing plants and trees on the land that bear fruit with seed in it, according to their various kinds.' And it was so. The land produced vegetation: plants bearing seed according to their kinds and trees bearing fruit with seed in it according to their kinds. And God saw that it was good."[8]

If we take this further, then we can delineate that "produce" typically refers to the raw or unprocessed agricultural output, while "product" refers to the processed or manufactured goods derived from that output. Unlike produce, products require rigorous process of making, manufacturing and packaging, involving, industrial, agricultural, and other means.

For instance, canned fruits, packaged bread, or dairy products like yoghurt. So, God, our creator categorically commanded us to bring forth, create and yield. Not only to produce, but to reproduce- constantly yielding and bring forth. "God blessed them: 'Prosper! Reproduce! Fill Earth! Take charge! Be responsible for fish in the sea and birds in the air, for every living thing that moves on the face of Earth.'"[9] By virtue of this command, we are all "producers." A producer is someone or something that creates or manufactures goods or services from produce.

Now, let's explore some examples of produce and

products across various careers:

Teachers for instance, cultivate a unique form of produce: their talent and gifting in a particular subject expertise, pedagogical strengths, and curriculum abilities. Through careful processing of this intellectual produce, they 'manufacture' graduates equipped with knowledge, create comprehensive educational resources, and develop engaging online courses. For graphic designers, they leverage their array of visual produce— their talents in visual aesthetics, design principles, colour palettes, among others. Subsequently, this aesthetic produce, when refined, results in cohesive brand identities, intuitive user interfaces, and eye-catching print publications.

Writers on the one hand nurture a literary produce of imagination, deep ideas, and their passion for research and character developments. This creative produce, once cultivated and polished, manifests as captivating novels, books, insightful journalistic pieces, and compelling screenplays. On the other hand, consultants cultivate their produce such as their analytical minds, strategic thinking and problem-solving giftings to yield products like comprehensive strategic plans, presentations, reports, transformative organizational restructures and improved business processes.

A few more examples to drive this home:

Architects through their produce comprising of the ability to think in three dimensions, creativity, passion for order and aesthetic appeal among others are able to create tangible products in the form of innovative buildings, harmonious urban plans, and functional interior spaces. How about Musicians? Through their pristine attention to detail, melodies, harmonies, and rhythmic patterns, they are able to cultivate them into recorded albums, energetic live performances, and emotive film scores.

For data scientists, their talents and giftings in problem-solving, with their analytical and curious mind, attention to detail, when processed, generates statistical models, algorithms, and data visualizations which in turn yields predictive analyses, and interactive business intelligence dashboards. How about fashion designers, their artistic ability, visual thinking and love for fabrics and style when brought to life, manifests as distinctive clothing collections, complementary accessories lines, and spectacular runway shows that set new trends in motion.

In each of these examples, the principle remains clear: as producers, we are tasked with transforming our raw 'produce' into the products and services that shape our world. Now, the next phase is production. Production is the phase of creating value distilled in products, commonly known as goods or services. What's the production process like? Well, like every production flow, there'd be an input of raw materials. Those are 'produce,' raw or unprocessed gifts, talents and abilities locked on our inside. Together with our activities- labour, information, creativity and innovation and hard work, they're processed into more valuable products. If you look closely, you'll see that activities alone without the produce may resort to mere busyness.

This is why a salesperson can be so busy but not productive because the activities are in isolation. There's no 'produce' attached with it. First, they aren't gifted for the path, so they struggle to fit in, but it remains a struggle. Next, they might spend hours making cold calls, sending emails, or attending networking events. However, if these activities don't result in actual sales or meaningful client relationships, it's just busyness.

True productivity for a salesperson would be measured in closed deals, revenue generated, or new long-term clients acquired. Remember that birds don't just fly, they actually love flying. It's hard to be productive without the initial release of the 'produce' in the equation.

Similarly, a manager might fill their day with meetings, but if these meetings don't lead to improved team performance, strategic decisions, or problem resolution, it's not productive. A productive manager would ensure that each meeting has clear objectives and outcomes that contribute to the team's or organization's goals. An artist could spend hours in their studio, but if they're not creating pieces that are ingenuine and excellent, resonating with their audience or advancing their artistic vision, they're busy but not necessarily productive.

An aspiring entrepreneur could attend numerous networking events, devour scores of business books, and continuously brainstorm ideas. Yet, without taking concrete steps to launch their business or validate their concept, it all amounts to mere busyness. Productive entrepreneurship requires diligent market research, meticulous crafting of a robust business plan and lean canvas, development of a minimum viable product, actively seeking feedback, and courageously taking calculated risks to bring innovative ideas to life.

This distinction between busyness and productivity is crucial in our modern work environment, where it's easy to confuse activity with achievement. It's not just about how many hours you work, but about the value and impact of your output. Therefore, productivity is the eventual measure of the efficiency of production. It measures how much output is produced per unit of input. Invariably, based on all that God has put inside of you, the inputs, He expects such a harvest of outputs. This first, must be sorted, how you can scale your personal productivity.

This reminds me of economic complexity, a measure of the knowledge in a society that gets translated into the products it makes. In the words of Cunningham, the most complex products are sophisticated chemicals and machinery, whereas the least complex products are raw materials or simple agricultural products. Now you see why we constantly need to go from produce to products. God provides the produce, your raw talents and gifts; those are part of the inputs. But next, you also provide part of it, through the quality of your activities, diligence and labour. I'll share more about this in the next section. Since God's portion of the input is met and constant, we are often negligent in supplying our own input.

Returning to the concept of economic complexity, we can see how this applies to individual careers as well. Just as nations strive to move from exporting raw materials to complex products, professionals should aim to evolve their skills and outputs. For instance, a data analyst might start by simply collecting and organizing data (produce), but over time, they should aim to provide complex predictive models and strategic insights (products) that drive business decisions. This progression from produce to products is not just about increasing complexity, but also about creating more value. It's about taking your raw talents and, through continuous learning and application, transforming them into high-value and high-income skills and outputs that solve complex problems or meet sophisticated needs.

Here's a graphic picture: "And he will be like a tree firmly planted and fed by streams of water, Which yields its fruit in its season; Its leaf does not wither; And in whatever he does, he prospers and comes to maturity."[10] So, if I refine my produce and follow methodical steps like we have it in photosynthesis for plants, then I can be sure to brings forth fruit in its due season. This is a beautiful reminder that productivity is not about instant results, but about consistent growth and development. Just as a tree takes time to grow strong and bear fruit, our productivity journey is one of continual refinement and maturation.

The blueprint of true productivity is about taking your God-given talents (your 'produce') and, through diligent effort and smart work (your 'activities'), creating valuable outputs (your 'products') that serve others and fulfil your purpose. This is how we truly answer the call to "Prosper! Reproduce! Fill Earth!" in our lives.

The Productivity Reflection Journal

Part 1: The Busyness vs. Productivity Challenge

How do you currently define "busyness" in your daily life?

What are some common tasks or activities you engage in that might be considered busyness rather than productivity?

_____

_____

_____

_____

_____

Mark the activities you often engage in that might be more "busy" than productive:

- [ ] Constantly checking emails

- [ ] Attending meetings without clear objectives

- [ ] Multitasking frequently

- [ ] Saying "yes" to every request

- [ ] Prioritizing urgent but unimportant tasks

- [ ] Other: _____

List at least three examples from your recent experiences where you were busy but not necessarily productive. Recall 3 recent examples:

Part 2: Unveiling True Productivity

How do you define "productivity" in the context of your work and personal life? What activities or outcomes do you consider as markers of true productivity?

What are 3 signs that show you're being productive in your career?:

List three examples where your activities led to meaningful results and demonstrated productivity. Share 3 instances where your efforts led to meaningful results:

Part 2: Your Productivity Goals

Based on your reflections, set three specific, measurable goals to improve and elevate your productivity:

Highest Learning Points

Take a moment to jot down and highlight the key insights and lessons that resonated with you most in this chapter.

Abraham O. Owoseni

Most Pressing Action Points

Take a moment to note down the key decisions and actions you would take based on the insights gained from this chapter.

Reproducing and Multiplying

Since our careers are likened to vehicles, some could decide to join and ride in existing vehicles while some others bring on new vehicles and others join them. Both are valuable, none is superior to the other or inferior to the other. It's about where we have found to produce more outputs, that matters. But sometimes, we often hear of people who complain of being stranded on the road due to limited vehicles to join. Could it be that those who could have produced 'new vehicles' have remained in existing vehicles? Please think deeply about this.

There's a mandate over our lives, please don't forget it. If you've mastered production to an extent, then get on to the next level: reproduction. As God commanded, "Prosper! Reproduce! Fill Earth! Take charge! Be responsible for fish in the sea and birds in the air, for every living thing that moves on the face of Earth.'" How do we realise this mandate? Here's one amazing way, illustrated through the biblical encounter between Elisha and the widow. In her desperation, her face etched with worry, she approached the prophet Elisha. Her voice trembles as she explains her dire situation. "My husband, who served the Lord faithfully, has passed away," she begins. "Now, the creditor threatens to take my two sons as slaves to settle our debt."

Elisha, moved by her plight, asks a simple yet profound question: "What do you have in your house?" This is the same question people often ask when they say, what can you do? What do you have? And by default, the easiest answer of least resistance is, 'nothing,' some others qualify it and say, 'nothing much.' But again, Elisha was asking a deep-seated question that had the power to foster production and reproduction. So, he asked with more emphasis, this time, he said, "What shall I do for you? Tell me, what do you have of value in the house?" The emphasis here is what value do you have? Based on your personal SWOT analysis, what strengths and opportunities are of value in your house-your life? That skill, that strength, that's your superpower. If Elisha had asked me, my response could have been, "Your servant has something in the house, he is good at teaching, making complex things simple; good in creating knowledge, and content that shapes the mind and he's good with communicating ideas and inspiring people. But see what the woman said, "Nothing," she says, "except a small jar of olive oil."

It's not about how much or plenty, but how you trade your value. In that moment, we saw the divine principle of multiplication at work. Elisha instructs her to borrow empty containers from her neighbours - not just a few, but as many as she can gather. Can you picture the scene? The widow and her sons, perhaps puzzled but trusting, went door to door, collecting jars of all shapes and sizes. I can imagine that she started production.

She converted the raw talent and gift she had into production, even though she called it, 'small.' Then came the moment of faith. Elisha tells her to go into her house, shut the door, and start pouring her small jar of oil into the borrowed containers. Don't just take this literally, this talks about exporting her produce, serving it to others, serving it to the world, creating businesses, and creating expressions out of her value. Do you see it now? As she begins to pour, something miraculous happens. The oil keeps flowing, defying natural laws, filling container after container.

Imagine the growing excitement in that small room! The

widow and her sons, their eyes wide with wonder, watching as the oil continues to flow. They keep bringing containers, and she keeps pouring, until finally, there are no more empty jars left. Then, the oil stopped flowing.

God is not only our source, but He also provides resources for multiplying and reproducing. Elisha's final instructions are equally important: "Go, sell the oil and pay your debt. You and your sons can live on the rest."[11] Multiplication is not just for our benefit, but also to meet our obligations and bless others, the kingdom and the global economy.

Remember, in our lives, we may often feel like we have only a "small jar of oil" - limited resources, talents, or opportunities. But when we offer what we have to God, trusting in His power to multiply, we can see miraculous results. Our "oil" - be it our skills, our time, or our resources - can be multiplied beyond our imagination when we align ourselves with God's purpose. So, I want to ask you, what "oil" do we have that God can multiply? Are we ready to step out in faith, gather our "empty containers," and watch as God fills them abundantly? Remember, in God's economy, multiplication starts with what we already have, no matter how small it may seem.

Personal SWOT Analysis Worksheet

Instructions

This personal SWOT (Strengths, Weaknesses, Opportunities, Threats) analysis is designed to help you identify your unique value - your "oil" - and consider how to multiply it. Follow these steps:

Be specific and honest in your responses. After completing all sections, review your answers and look for patterns or insights. Create an action plan based on your analysis.

Strengths (Your "Oil")

In this section, identify your unique talents, skills, and positive attributes. These are your assets, your "oil" that can be multiplied. *(See the Potent-Intent worksheet in the next chapter for more immersive guide)*

- What unique skills or talents do you possess?
- What do others often compliment you on?
- What experiences or knowledge sets you apart?
- What personal qualities do you have that add value?

Weaknesses (Areas for Growth)

Assess areas where you struggle or need improvement. Recognizing these can help you plan for growth and development.

- What tasks do you often avoid or struggle with?
- What skills do you lack that might be holding you back?
- What personal traits might limit your effectiveness?

Opportunities (Empty Containers)

This section is about identifying potential areas for growth, application of your strengths, or new directions. These are your "*empty containers*" waiting to be filled.

- What trends in your field could you leverage?
- What networks or relationships could you develop?
- What new skills could amplify your existing strengths?
- What unmet needs exist that align with your strengths?

Threats (Challenges to Overcome)

Consider external factors or personal limitations that could hinder your progress or success.

- What obstacles might prevent you from utilizing your strengths?
- Are there external factors that could limit your growth?
- What competition exists in your area of expertise?

Self-Discovery Questions

Use these questions to gain deeper insights from your analysis:

1. How can you "*pour your oil*" (use your strengths) in new ways?

---

2. What "*empty containers*" (opportunities) can you gather to expand your impact?

3. How might your weaknesses be transformed into strengths?

4. What steps can you take to mitigate potential threats?

Action Plan

Based on your SWOT analysis, outline 3-5 concrete steps you can take to multiply your "oil" and create more value:

"Multiplication starts with what we already have, no matter how small it may seem."

Highest Learning Points

Take a moment to jot down and highlight the key insights and lessons that resonated with you most in this chapter.

Most Pressing Action Points

Take a moment to note down the key decisions and actions you would take based on the insights gained from this chapter.

Personal Productivity and National Productivity —The Ripple Effect

I once moderated a National Budget Roundtable and Panel Discussion hosted by the Centre for Economic Policy and Development Research (CEPDeR). One of the keynote speakers, a Special Adviser to the President on economic affairs, Dr. Tola Fasau expounded on the Product Space drawing insights from the work of Harvard Professor Ricardo Hausmann, the Founder and Director of Harvard's Growth Lab.

Talking about the product space and the universe of productivity, every country is as productive as its citizens and workforce. If a country is playing in more product space means that there are many talents and workforce in that product space. Let's look at this closely: the product space illustrates how countries can diversify and upgrade their production capabilities over time. For instance, South Africa has diversified its economy beyond traditional commodities like minerals into sectors such as automotive manufacturing and financial services. South Korea transformed from a low-income agricultural economy to a high-tech powerhouse by focusing on the electronics and automotive industries. Germany is renowned for its manufacturing prowess, exporting high-value products such as automobiles, machinery, and precision instruments. Chile has improved its economic complexity by diversifying from mainly copper exports to include more processed goods and services. The United States has a high economic complexity due to its diverse range of exports, from advanced technology to agricultural products.[12]

If personal productivity is sorted, then we can scale the conversation to what Shawn Cunningham calls, "The productive structure of an economy." Invariably, to change the national productive structure, he opines that it would take both public and private focus on building the right kinds of institutions, like organizations, policies and informal institutions, for example, leading a cultural change.[13]

Now, imagine you can see the import and impact of your work beyond your current horizon. Imagine your productivity level can soar and take a leap. Then, you can see how you can contribute more effectively to economic growth. With each one playing their part through their discovered God-given purposes and lifework whether in professional careers, vocational or entrepreneurial careers, we can have a thriving ecosystem that fosters innovation, and effectiveness, and ultimately contributes to the country's expansion in its product space. As more individuals become productive in their respective product spaces, they collectively enhance their country's economic complexity. This leads to increased competitiveness, job creation, and overall prosperity as the economy diversifies and moves into more advanced industries.

In a subsequent chapter, I'll share the case studies of Joseph and, Daniel, but first, let's explore the production process.

Abraham O. Owoseni

Highest Learning Points

Take a moment to jot down and highlight the key insights and lessons that resonated with you most in this chapter.

Most Pressing Action Points

Take a moment to note down the key decisions and actions you would take based on the insights gained from this chapter.

The Production Process: A Seven-Step Guide

The Production Process

I was training an audience recently on creativity and innovation, and I noted that creativity is not reserved for "*creative people.*" We often confine creativity to specific fields, but in reality, everyone possesses this ability. I'll demonstrate how shortly. Just as every factory and production plant operates with a well-defined production line, creativity and innovation act as the process for transforming raw produce into valuable products. What exactly does this process entail? Let's explore it comprehensively:

First and foremost, identify and articulate your *produce*—your innate gifts, talents, and abilities. If you are uncertain of this, then you can explore the Potent-Intent Worksheet to help you articulate them.

Reflection Worksheet: Potent-Intent Starter

This worksheet will guide you through a deep exploration of your potential. It has three parts with three major prompts to guide you in unveiling your true potential. Take your time, reflect deeply, and get ready to unlock your true potential!

Part 1: Discover Your "Good At"s

1. What am I good at?

[Clue: What actions do you find replenishing & re-invigorating when you do them? For example, speaking, teaching, writing, analyzing, creating, solving problems, organizing, designing, inspiring others, and more.

Make a list of them: Start with the words, 'I'm good at...'

I'm good at:

I'm good at:

I'm good at:

I'm good at:

To help you draw out more thoughts and responses on this question, reflect on the following additional questions:

Action Energizers: What are those activities that leave you feeling replenished and re-energized; you naturally gravitate towards and enjoy doing them.

Make a list of them: [Start with the words, 'I'm good at...']

I'm good at:

Activity Spotlight: Think of activities you've been praised for or come easily to you. These are areas where you excel and can bring value to others. (For instance, communication, organization, critical thinking).

Make a list of them: [Start with the words, 'I'm good at...']

I'm good at:

Flow Zone: Recall moments when you were completely immersed in an activity and lost track of time. What were you doing? This is your flow zone, where your talents shine brightest.

Make a list of them: [Start with the words, 'I'm good at...']

I'm good at:

Part 2: Discover Your "Good With"s

2. What am I good with?

[Clue: This can be attributes you demonstrate and display physically. For instance, one person could be good with people, while another is good with children or good with money, some others are good with managing time, collaborating, leading, nurturing and so on. Think deeply and make a list of them:

Start with the words, 'I'm good with...'

I'm good with

I'm good with

I'm good with

To help you draw out more thoughts and responses on this question, reflect on the following additional questions:

People Magnet: What groups or individuals do you naturally connect with? What qualities do you possess that draw them in? (e.g., empathy, humour, leadership, etc.) Make a list of them: [Start with the words, 'I'm good with...']

I'm good with

Physical Prowess: Are you naturally coordinated, resourceful, or adaptable in physical settings? What physical attributes do you possess that set you apart? (e.g., strength, dexterity, spatial awareness, etc.) Make a list of them: [Start with the words, 'I'm good with...']

I'm good with

Relational Intelligence: What skills do you possess in navigating relationships and fostering emotional well-being? (e.g., active listening, conflict resolution, self-awareness, etc.) Make a list of them: [Start with the words, 'I'm good with...']

I'm good with

Part 3: Discover Your "Good In"s

3. What am I good in?

[Clue: This could be school subjects you excelled in naturally. It also includes fields of knowledge you're very passionate about. For instance, someone could be very good in mathematics, science, business, technology, arts, language and literature, psychology, social sciences or humanities. Think deeply and make a list of them:
Start with the words, 'I'm good in...'

I'm good in

I'm good in

I'm good in

To help you draw out more thoughts and responses on this question, reflect on the following additional questions:
Natural Gravitations: What subjects or fields of knowledge have always fascinated you? What topics, courses, or subjects did you instinctively gravitate towards so far in your learning adventure and in school? (e.g., history, science, art) Make a list of them: [Start with the words, 'I'm good in...']

I'm good in

Passion Projects: What activities or pursuits spark your inner fire and make you feel truly alive? These are your passion projects, areas where your natural talents and interests intersect. (e.g., creative writing, volunteering, entrepreneurship)

Make a list of them: [Start with the words, 'I'm good in...']

I'm good in

Knowledge and Inclination: What impact do you want to make on the world? What skills and knowledge have you found yourself inclined to even though you haven't gone to school to study them? For instance, someone who is naturally inclined towards understanding and experimenting with new technologies and innovations, environmental sustainability, and conservation efforts, mental health and well-being, graphic design, and visual arts, DIY crafting, and handmade arts, or community building and networking, entrepreneurship, and business strategy and so on. Think about yours and make a list of them:

Start with the words, 'I'm good in...'

I'm good in

Congratulations! Imagine all these treasures within you,

Now, take a moment to write them out again and see your unique potential at a glance. Then, reflect on how each gift can be purposefully used to achieve your career goals and how they work together to shape your career journey.

Potent	Intent
What specific gifts, talents, and abilities have you identified in yourself?	What are you meant to use these gifts, talents, and abilities for in achieving your career goals?
List out all the "I'm good at"	

List out all the "I'm good with"

List out all the "I'm good in"

I was well coached by the productivity maestro, Remi Dairo, a US-based productivity expert and I like his mantra: "Productivity is the most important thing on earth—increasing the capacity of human resources and other factors for maximum result with less and without stress!" Now, to increase your capacity, what if you know what makes the production process?

Like I shared, just like every factory operates with a defined production line, creativity and innovation are the vital processes that transform raw talents and abilities into valuable products. Now that you've identified your raw produce through your gifts and talents, it's time to catalyse them into novel products and services. This is where creativity and innovation come into play. And remember, these aren't skills reserved for a select few; everyone can cultivate and harness them. You can stir up your creativity.

To distinguish between the two terms: Creativity initiates the production journey—it's the process of generating ideas. It sets the stage for innovation, which is the productive process of implementing those ideas. I love how one of my mentors put it, Dr. Gbenga Alalade, the Project Director and

Lead Architect of 'The Ark Legacy Project'—a 100,000-seat stadium-like sanctuary for Winners Chapel International, Canaanland, poised to be the world's largest covered stadium upon completion. He said, "Leaders start with creativity but thrive with innovation as they continuously evolve. Leaders become ineffective when they stop at creativity. Effective

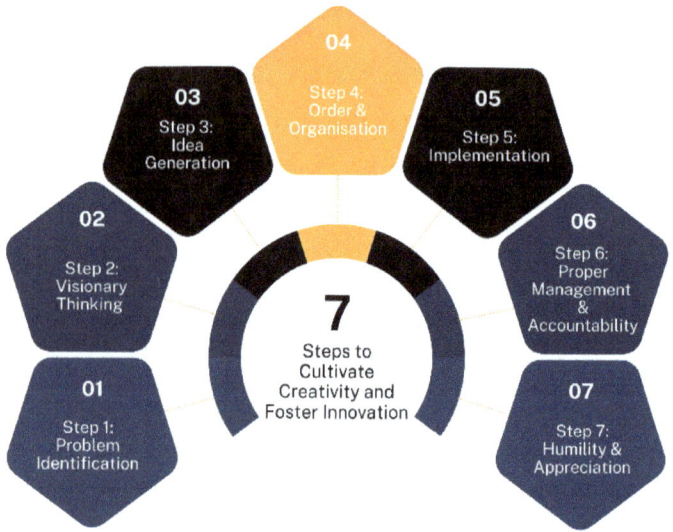

leaders are the ones who are innovative." So, how can you begin to cultivate creativity and foster innovation? Let's explore the practical steps:

Figure 1: 7 Steps to Cultivate Creativity and Foster Innovation
Source: Owoseni A.O. (2024)

Step 1: Problem Identification

Creativity finds its inspiration in the corridors of the

problems we feel passionately about addressing. There are two key aspects to identifying these problems. Firstly, consider the enduring challenges. You've already identified your 'produce'—your natural abilities and giftings—but it's crucial to be acutely aware of the specific problems they are destined to solve. This awareness will keep you at the forefront of innovation throughout your career journey. Secondly, there are the everyday work challenges. Many professionals tend to avoid these, opting for the path of least resistance. However, these challenges often hold the seeds of new ideas. Problems are not obstacles; they exist to push us beyond our comfort zones.

Reflecting on everyday work challenges, I recall the impact of the global pandemic in 2020, in-person conferences and events were disrupted worldwide. I was serving in the central committee as a sub-chair for a bi-annual flagship conference at the time. Before that time, the conference held solely on-site with participants- policymakers and influential stakeholders from government, industry, academia, the private sector, and financial institutions, traveling down to the conference site. So here we were faced with a problem, the global lockdown.

The easiest supposed solution was to cancel the year's edition. But the best way to make more impact and novelty will be when we approach problems with an optimistic mindset. So, I made considerable contributions, thanks to the leadership of my chair, who gave me the free will to bring up several creative ideas which were implemented, and we hosted the first ever virtual edition. Today, virtual and hybrid conferences have become a global norm. Talking about the first pillar of problem, what problems have you identified to solve on the long haul leveraging the produce God's given to you?

The creation of the earth started out as a problem but soon became a masterpiece of innovation. What happened? The earth was without form and void, "It was without shape and empty, and darkness was over the surface of the watery deep, but the Spirit of God was moving over the surface of the water"[14] It was a problem no doubt, but God continued to work. Problems shouldn't deter us; they should stir us to unleash creative ideas. Dr. Sam Adeyemi, leadership expert and author of *Dear Leader*, puts it this way: "Don't run away from problems; leverage them as opportunities to experience shifts to a new level. That's what gives you big shifts and big jumps in life."

Ask yourself, "Of all human needs, which one(s) has been a longing concern for me? What problem has this concern brought as a result? Which set of people does the problem affect? Think deeply about these questions to identify the problems. Identifying a broad concern can lead to pinpointing specific problems and the groups of people most affected by them. This process of defining the problem is indeed a crucial first step in channeling your passion and 'produce,' into meaningful, creative solutions. If you haven't identified the specific problem yet, at least identify the concern. My preferable trio is for you to know the concern that is a big burden for you and the problems emanating from it and those it affects. To get you started, take a look at these random examples.

Consider the concern of inclusive design, where inaccessible public spaces pose significant challenges for people with disabilities. This problem poses a persistent barrier in everyday environments. Their exclusion calls for urgent need for innovative solutions that promote universal accessibility. Likewise, sustainable transportation is a critical concern amidst rising urbanization. Vehicular emissions contribute to air pollution, posing serious health risks, particularly to urban residents, especially those with respiratory issues. Addressing this problem requires initiatives that prioritize cleaner transport alternatives and urban planning strategies that prioritize public health.

How about youth unemployment stemming from a skill mismatch. Recent graduates and young job seekers often struggle to find suitable employment opportunities that align with their qualifications. Bridging this gap demands proactive efforts in education reform, vocational training, and fostering partnerships between academia and industries. Digital literacy is another pressing concern in our increasingly digital world. Limited access to technology education affects older adults and rural populations, hindering their ability to fully participate in the digital economy and access essential services online. Promoting digital literacy initiatives can empower these groups and bridge the digital divide.

The urban landscape itself presents its own set of challenges. The transition to renewable energy is imperative in mitigating climate change, yet many communities remain dependent on fossil fuels. Vulnerable communities, disproportionately affected by climate change impacts, urgently require sustainable energy solutions to enhance resilience and environmental sustainability.

Digital privacy concerns are increasingly pertinent in a data-driven age, with data breaches and identity theft affecting internet users, particularly those with limited tech knowledge. Strengthening digital privacy laws and promoting cybersecurity awareness are critical steps in safeguarding personal information and ensuring online safety. Access to healthcare is a fundamental human right, yet high medical costs create barriers for uninsured and underinsured individuals. Addressing this concern involves advocating for healthcare reforms that prioritize affordability, accessibility, and equitable healthcare delivery.

In agriculture, sustainable practices are essential to combat soil degradation, which adversely affects small-scale farmers and rural communities' livelihoods. Promoting sustainable agriculture methods can enhance soil health, increase crop yields, and ensure food security for future generations. Substance abuse prevention is critical amid the opioid crisis, affecting rural communities and at-risk youth disproportionately. Combating substance abuse requires comprehensive strategies that include education, treatment programs, and community support initiatives to address addiction and promote recovery.

Food security remains a challenge, particularly in urban food deserts where low-income families lack access to affordable and nutritious food options. Addressing food deserts involves community-based initiatives, urban agriculture projects, and policy interventions to ensure equitable access to healthy food choices.

Now, think about these questions again and note your

thoughts:

Ask yourself:

Of all human needs, which one(s) has been a longing concern for me?

What problem has this concern brought as a result?

Which set of people does the problem affect? Think deeply about these questions to identify the problems. Identifying a broad concern can lead to pinpointing specific problems and the groups of people most affected by them.

In addressing these concerns and problems, defining the issues clearly is the crucial first step. In identifying these issues and the groups they affect, you can also uncover opportunities for innovation, compassion, and positive change.

What do you See?

My most revered role model, the Lt Dr Myles Munroe would say, "Everything we need to change our world, our countries, businesses and communities exist now. Everything needed to invent the next new thing is already present. Innovation is what you think about what you have." He went further to emphasise that, "Eyes that look are common, eyes that see are rare. Some look at sheep, others see shoes and clothing; some look a wheat, others see a bakery."

Some look at a pile of discarded plastic bottles and see trash, while others envision eco-friendly building materials. When faced with food waste, most see a disposal problem. Innovators, however, see potential for biodegradable packaging materials or renewable energy through biogas production. Some look at roof spaces and see unused areas, while solar energy innovators see potential power plants and urban farming opportunities.

What do you see?

Innovation involves seeing possibilities beyond the obvious and leveraging existing resources in novel ways to create transformative solutions that meet and solve evolving needs and challenges in our society.

Traditional media companies focused on broadcasting TV and radio programs. Innovators saw the opportunity to stream content directly to consumers through platforms like Netflix, and YouTube revolutionizing how content is shared. Retailers saw physical stores as the primary means to sell products. Innovators envisioned e-commerce platforms like Amazon,

Shopify, WooCommerce which transformed the retail industry by offering a vast selection of goods online with convenient delivery options. Some saw underutilized assets like spare rooms or cars. Innovators saw the potential to create platforms like Airbnb and Uber, leveraging shared resources to provide lodging and transportation services more efficiently. Companies saw offices as the standard workplace. Innovators saw the opportunity to develop tools like Zoom and Slack, enabling seamless communication and collaboration for remote teams worldwide.

Again, I'll like to ask, what do you see?

This takes us to the next step:

Step 2: Visionary Thinking

Recall that the first step was to identify the problem; The next step is to join the 10% who don't just talk about the problems; they give thoughtful consideration to them. In doing so, we begin to demonstrate visionary and innovative thinking—looking beyond the immediate challenges, imagining new possibilities. This process requires a mental environment characterized by quietness, calmness, and curiosity. Mentally speaking, you cannot solve a problem from within the problem itself.

The goal at this stage is not to immediately find practical solutions, but to open our minds to the realm of possibility. We're training ourselves to see potential where others see obstacles, to envision abundance where others see scarcity. Asking "what if?" without immediately constraining with "how?" It's about giving ourselves permission to dream boldly and think radically. For its only by first imagining a better world that we can begin to create one.

Step 3: Idea Generation

The next line of production is the generation of ideas; as you begin to brood on the problems, envisioning possibilities, ideas are birth. "The Spirit of God was moving (hovering, brooding) over the face of the waters (upon the situation). [15] To brood is to be engaged in or showing deep thought about something. You do this with your entire faculty- spirit, soul and body. "For there's a spirit in man for stirring ideas."[16]

Step 4: Order and Organisation

To excel in your career, it's crucial to maintain order both physically and digitally, especially when it comes to understanding and addressing the problems you aim to solve. Take the time to thoroughly grasp the situation at hand. Gather primary, authentic data and analyse it meticulously to unearth insights that can inspire ideas and guide informed decisions.

In lean manufacturing, this concept is likened to the visual workplace principle—a method that emphasizes visually appealing and easily accessible workspaces to optimize production efficiency. Imagine this: if you spend five minutes searching for a file on your computer or in a cluttered shelf, it may seem insignificant, but it can disrupt your production flow significantly.

One of the things Jesus did when He was about to feed the people after He identified the problem and empathised with them. It was a problematic scene already; the people were hungry. "When Jesus looked out and saw that a large crowd had arrived, he said to Philip, "Where can we buy bread to feed these people?" He said this to stretch Philip's faith. He already knew what he was going to do." [17] Philip answered, "Someone would have to work almost a year to buy enough bread for each person here to have only a little piece."[18] That's the thing with creativity, it starts with an open wide audacious mindset.

You can't be creative if you're always pessimistic. Everything is possible, anything is possible. Another follower there was Andrew. He was Simon Peter's brother. Andrew said, "Here is a boy with five loaves of barley bread and two little fish. But that is not enough for so many people."[19] Even though you have an idea, you need organisation, so the ideas don't get muddled up. Write them down, have a physical and digital repository to document them, and step -by-step progress. Jesus said, "Tell the people to sit down." This was a very grassy place. There were about 5,000 men who sat down there. Then Jesus took the loaves of bread. He thanked God for the bread and gave it to the people who were sitting there. He did the same with the fish. He gave them as much as they wanted. They all had enough to eat.

When they had finished, Jesus said to his followers, "Gather the pieces of fish and bread that were not eaten. Don't waste anything." So they gathered up the pieces that were left. They filled 12 large baskets with the pieces that were left of the five barley loaves.[20] Build structure around your schedule and routine to continually flow in creativity. Create allowances for momentous Ideas- sudden ideas that emanate from places, people and providence. Even if you haven't executed all ideas, have them in view, well documented, and don't waste anything.

Step 5: Implementation

Implementation starts from the non-physical to the physical, "Then, God said, let there be light and there was light!"[21] So you can agree with God to birth and implement your novel creative ideas. "By faith we understand that the worlds were framed by the word of God, so that the things which are seen were not made of things which are visible."[22] As great as ideas are, they're hardly celebrated, innovations are. Innovations are simply, implemented ideas. Before our first In-School Youth Development Centre was established in 2014, I saw it, and believed it. It had been established before it was built. I spoke about it in videos and interviews, "Word-created then, physically manifested. That's the straight-line equation. Don't wait for perfect conditions. Many years ago, I came across this insight from Dr. John Maxwell's book, "Put Your Dream to the Test," in it, he said, "If you don't start pursuing your dream now, next year, you will only be a year older and not a step closer to it." That sank so deep into my subconscious and continually fuels my intrinsic motivation. What's your big dream? What are your big ideas? When will you start implementing them? Are you only going to cut cakes on your next birthday and take beautiful pictures alone? Will you be a step closer or just a year older to your big dreams this year?

Leverage what you have; as Dr. Myles noted, innovation isn't about inventing something from nothing, but rather about perceiving the hidden potential in what already exists. It's about transforming the ordinary into the extraordinary through the power of vision and creative thinking. As he suggests, the key lies not just in looking, but truly seeing - recognizing the latent possibilities in our surroundings and having the courage to bring those possibilities to life.

Step 6: Proper Management and Accountability

Creative ideas are like seeds; each idea has the potential to germinate into fruits of innovation. As such, every creative idea targeted at solving any identified problem for human good is to be highly cherished and accounted for. Of the ideas God gave you, which ones have you executed? Which ones are in progress? Do you have a journal to track them, have you phased them? Which ones are for this quarter? When God sees you as a good steward of the creative ideas He gives you, then, He sends you more. "He also who had received the one talent came forward, saying, 'Master, I knew you to be a hard man, reaping where you did not sow, and gathering where you scattered no seed, so I was afraid, and I went and hid your talent in the ground. Here, you have what is yours.' But his master answered him, 'You wicked and slothful servant! You knew that I reap where I have not sown and gather where I scattered no seed? So take the talent from him and give it to him who has the ten talents."[23]

Step 7: Humility and Appreciation

I know how it feels in the corporate world, everyone is looking to attribute the praise, "I did it," "If it wasn't for my input," "It was my idea," and so on. First, this stifles teamwork, when an individual is aiming to 'take the glory,' so he assumes to work all alone, so no one can 'share the glory' with him. There's hardly much that can be achieved that way. "Together, Everyone Achieves More!" That's the spirit of a T.E.A.M. Yes, we all do our individual work, team-work is a concerted effort of more than one person to achieve greater output and production. Even a plane requires a pilot and a co-pilot to fly. A marriage requires a man and woman in holy matrimony, a family requires two parents, each player contributes their skills and strengths, and success to win a match. In music, each member plays a vital role, and the collective effort enhances the overall performance to create harmonious music.

Medical teams of doctors, nurses, and specialists work together provide comprehensive care to patients. Architects, engineers, contractors, and others contributes expertise to complete complex projects successfully. Directors, producers, actors, cinematographers, and crew member collaborate to bring a story to life on screen. Teachers, administrators, and support staff in schools collaborate to create a conducive learning environment for students. All departments collaborate on project goals to drive innovation, productivity, and business growth.

"Joseph answered Pharaoh, saying, "It is not in me to interpret the dream; God not I will give Pharaoh a favorable answer through me.""[24] One of my childhood experiences was a television series called "Super Story" by WAP TV. It aired on Thursdays at 8 PM and it was arguably one of the memorable series back in the days. As part of the close out scenes of the programme, these words are reechoed, "We are nothing but pencils in the hand of the creator." It was so hard to forget those words; we're vessels, I am a vessel, so you are.

"Does this mean we can't celebrate our wins?" Absolutely not, we can. But as we do, we return the glory to the source. The creative ideas were given to you. Not only that, you were also able to execute them. Not everyone could execute their ideas. The ideas were a gift, remember. "What makes you better than anyone else? What do you have that was not given to you? If it was given to you, why do you brag as if you did not receive it as a gift?"[25] This book for instance isn't mine, it was a gift. I'm only the vessel of its passage to the world. I couldn't have figured out all the ideas and insights with my limited mind. God is the source through the help of the Holy Spirit. This chapter isn't me, but the Lord Jesus. I couldn't just finish it through, He kept bringing more ideas to enrich it, till He gave me the clearance to go to the next. What humility and appreciation does to God is to rip off the urges of pride. "God resists you when you are proud but continually pours out grace when you are humble."[26]

In summary, the first stage in this production process is to identify and articulate your "produce"—your innate gifts, talents, and abilities. Next, you engage creativity and innovation to transform this raw produce into valuable products. Dr. Stephen Oluwatobi, AI leader, growth lead, leadership coach, and strategist, offers a similar perspective: "It is not your resources, but your resourcefulness, that determines the worth of your life. As you live your life, pay attention to what you're able to create and produce with your talents and resources. Your product is the outcome of your resourcefulness—it is your packaged value, shipped to receive value in exchange. It is not your fruit, but your fruitfulness, that makes you."

Highest Learning Points

Take a moment to jot down and highlight the key insights and lessons that resonated with you most in this chapter.

Abraham O. Owoseni

Most Pressing Action Points

Take a moment to note down the key decisions and actions you would take based on the insights gained from this chapter.

Abraham O. Owoseni

The Remarkable Productivity of Joseph and Daniel

How has this experience been for you through this book? I have fulfilled my role and delivered my assignment. Now, it's your turn to take action. I eagerly anticipate hearing your testimonies of productive labour and significant achievements.

I have always admired Poju Oyemade, the founder and senior pastor of The Covenant Nation (TCN), for his innovative drive and openness to embracing technology and other media to spread the gospel of Jesus Christ. I once heard him say, "Don't ask for favour, ask for productivity." He illustrated this with the example of Joseph, who was promoted by Potiphar not because of a request for favour, but because

Potiphar observed Joseph's remarkable productivity. Despite starting as a housekeeper, everything Joseph did prospered. Potiphar had no choice but to promote him to become manager of his entire household. This level of productivity, even in a role as a slave, paved the way for Joseph's future impact, influence, and prosperity, eventually making him the Prime Minister of Egypt. Similarly, Daniel was noted for being ten times better, reflecting the same principle of exceptional productivity.

As we conclude the experience shared in this book, I want to emphasize these two relatable case studies from scripture: Joseph and Daniel. Let's closely examine these examples to understand their profound principles of productivity.

1. Joseph: From Slave to Prime Minister

1.1 Background

Joseph was the eleventh son of Jacob, born to Rachel in Canaan. A key figure in the Bible and known for his extraordinary rise from being a slave to becoming the Prime Minister of Egypt.

> "Joseph was a much-loved son, the favourite of his father Jacob, set apart from his brothers. But when his brothers saw that their father loved him more than the others,

they grew to hate him and couldn't say a kind word to him."[27]

Joseph's life story demonstrates how God can use even the most challenging circumstances to unlock unprecedented productivity and impact. When faced with adversity, such as being sold into slavery and wrongfully imprisoned, Joseph did not allow these setbacks to define him. Instead, he maintained a posture of faith, diligence, and innovative thinking.

He went ahead to interpret Pharaoh's dream and proposed a strategic plan to address the impending famine. Rather than simply predicting the crisis, Joseph offered a comprehensive solution that involved organizing a large-scale production and storage system.[28] This proactive, problem-solving mindset allowed Joseph to transform a looming disaster into an opportunity for prosperity. The same productive mindset he had while in Potiphar's house is the same one that birthed a global solution. This serves as a reminder to protect your productive mindset your productive mindset; it's the wellspring of your prosperity.

Now, as a result of his productivity and stewardship, "the whole world came to Egypt to Joseph to buy grain, because the famine was severe over all the earth"[29] Joseph's ability to thrive in the midst of adversity and provide innovative solutions catapulted him into a position of immense influence, ultimately elevating his personal productivity and that of the nation.

1.2 Key Events and Principles

Here are some principles from the key events from Joseph's work and life journey:

1. **Visionary Thinking**: Leveraging on the gifts and abilities God had endowed him, he was able to interpret Pharaoh's dream, like he had always done. But he didn't stop there, he plugged his produce—his innate gifts, talents, and abilities into a bigger vision, not only for himself but for the nation and neighbouring nations.

"Then Joseph said to Pharaoh, 'The dreams of Pharaoh are one and the same. God has revealed to Pharaoh what he is about to do. The seven good cows are seven years, and the seven good heads of grain are seven years; it is one and the same dream. The seven thin, ugly cows that came up afterward are seven years, and the seven worthless heads of grain scorched by the east wind are also seven years of famine. It is just as I said to Pharaoh: God has shown Pharaoh what he is about to do. Seven years of great abundance are coming throughout the land of Egypt, but seven years of famine will follow them. Then all the abundance in Egypt will be forgotten, and the famine will ravage the land. The abundance in the land will not be remembered, because the famine that follows it will be so severe. The reason the dream was given to Pharaoh in two forms is that the matter has been firmly decided by God, and God will do it soon."[30]

2. **Problem Identification**: Next, Joseph quickly identified the core problem at hand - the impending famine that could devastate Egypt and surrounding nations.

"But there will come seven years of famine and hunger, and all the [previous] plenty will be forgotten in the land of Egypt; and the famine will exhaust (consume and make an end of) the land."[31]

This reinforces the resolve to be courageous at any given problem; it's an opportunity to create solutions. Don't hate problems, hate the negative impact they have and love the solutions that would emerge when they're solved or mitigated.

3. **Creative Solution Generation**: Rather than simply predicting the crisis, Joseph offers a comprehensive

solution that involves organizing a large-scale production and storage system.

> "My suggestion is that you find the wisest man in Egypt and put him in charge of administering a nationwide farm program. Let Pharaoh divide Egypt into five administrative districts, and let the officials of these districts gather into the royal storehouses all the excess crops of the next seven years, so that there will be enough to eat when the seven years of famine come. Otherwise, disaster will surely strike."[32]

Many discuss and analyse the problem, they diagnose the problems without iterating for solutions. Rather, choose to think solutions, think way outs, make recommendations and be a contribution-driven leader.

4. **Implementation and Management**: Joseph is appointed to oversee the implementation of his plan, showcasing his ability to move from idea to action. Break the inertia and move past ideas to implementation. The fear is not

real, *"false evidence appearing real,"* what will people say, the fear of getting rejected or mocked? "What if it fails," you say, What if it doesn't work? Due to his productive mindset, he was entrusted with the responsibility of implementing the recommendations he had proposed. His ability to think creatively and strategically not only earned him this significant role but also demonstrated his capability to drive meaningful outcomes. This appointment was a direct result of his innovative approach and effective problem-solving skills.

> "Joseph's suggestions were well received by Pharaoh and his assistants. As they discussed who should be appointed for the job, Pharaoh said, "Who could do it better than Joseph? For he is a man who is obviously filled with the Spirit of God." Turning to Joseph, Pharaoh said to him, "Since God has revealed the meaning of the dreams to you, you are the wisest man in the country! I am hereby appointing you to be in charge of this entire project. What you say goes, throughout all the land of Egypt. I alone will outrank you."[33]

5. **Accountability and Stewardship**: Now, see how careful stewardship and accountability sustained the impact of Joseph's breakthrough-Joseph's careful management ensured that Egypt not only survived the famine but became a resource

for other nations.

> "So when the famine had spread over the whole country, Joseph opened all the storehouses and sold grain to the Egyptians, for the famine was severe throughout Egypt. And all the world came to Egypt to buy grain from Joseph, because the famine was severe everywhere."[34]

1.3 Lessons for Modern Productivity:

1. **Resilience in Adversity**: Joseph's journey shows us how setbacks can actually pave the way for future success. Imagine you're working on a big project and encounter a major obstacle, like losing a crucial client or facing a significant technical failure. Instead of letting these setbacks derail you, view them as opportunities to learn and grow. Just as Joseph turned his time in prison into a stepping stone to become a powerful leader, you can use your challenges to build new skills, rethink your approach, and come out stronger.

2. **Strategic Foresight**: Joseph's ability to interpret the dream and devise a long-term plan demonstrates the importance of strategic thinking in productivity. This relates to the concept of "strategic foresight" in management theory, which emphasizes the ability to anticipate future challenges

and opportunities.[35] In your daily life, this might look like creating a financial cushion for unexpected expenses or developing new skills to stay relevant in your career. For example, if you're in a rapidly changing field like technology, investing time in learning about emerging trends or new tools can keep you ahead of the curve. Strategic foresight means not just reacting to problems as they arise but anticipating them and being prepared. It means, thinking long-range! Productive leaders don't limit their ideas and actions to the present, they think long-range.

3. **Systems Thinking**: Joseph's solution involved creating a comprehensive system for food production, storage, and distribution. This reflects the principles of systems thinking, which involves understanding how different parts of a system interrelate and how systems work over time and within the context of larger systems.[36] Think of a project where you're managing several tasks and team members. Systems thinking involves looking at how each part of the project affects the others. For example, if you're planning a marketing campaign, consider how each component—social media, email newsletters, and advertising—interacts with and impacts the others. By seeing the bigger picture and understanding these interactions, you can create a more cohesive and effective

strategy.

2. Daniel: Excellence in a Foreign Land

2.1 Background

Daniel was a young Jewish noble who was taken into captivity by Nebuchadnezzar, the king of Babylon. Despite being uprooted from his homeland and placed in a foreign environment with unfamiliar customs and beliefs, Daniel remained steadfast in his faith and integrity. This unwavering commitment became the cornerstone of his extraordinary productivity and influence. He overcame intense political and religious challenges by excelling in his duties, showcasing remarkable problem-solving skills, and maintaining his principles.

2.2 Key Events and Principles

Here are some principles from the key events from Daniel's work and life journey:

1. **Principled Living**: Daniel's refusal to eat the king's food to stay true to his faith shows his commitment to his principles. This choice demonstrates how living by your values can guide your decisions and actions, even in challenging environments.

"But Daniel was determined not to defile himself by eating the food and wine given to them by the king. He asked the chief of staff for permission not to eat these unacceptable foods. Now God had given the chief of staff a special appreciation for Daniel.

But he was alarmed by Daniel's request and said, 'I am afraid of my lord the king, who has ordered that you be given this food and wine. If you become pale and thin compared to the other youths your age, I am afraid the king will have me beheaded.'

Daniel spoke with the attendant who had been appointed by the chief of staff to look after Daniel, Hananiah, Mishael, and Azariah. 'Please test us for ten days on a diet of vegetables and water,' Daniel said. 'Then compare our appearance with the other young men who are eating the king's food, and base your decision on what you see.'

The attendant agreed to Daniel's suggestion and tested them for ten days. And at the end of the ten days, Daniel and his three friends looked healthier and better nourished than the young men who had been eating the royal food."[40]

2. **Continuous Learning**: Daniel and his companions

excelled in their studies, reflecting their commitment to continuous learning and personal growth. Their dedication to acquiring knowledge enabled them to stand out and succeed.

> "As for these four youths, God gave them knowledge and skill in all learning and wisdom; and Daniel had understanding in all kinds of visions and dreams. At the end of the time which the king had set for bringing them in, the chief of the king's attendants brought them in before Nebuchadnezzar. When the king talked with them, he found them ten times better than all the learned magicians and enchanters who were in his whole realm."[41]

3. **Divine Wisdom**: Faced with the challenge of interpreting Nebuchadnezzar's dream, Daniel turns to prayer for guidance and receives supernatural insight. This highlights the value of seeking wisdom and support beyond your own understanding. (Daniel 2:17-19).

> "Then Daniel went home and told his three friends, Hananiah, Mishael, and Azariah, about the king's demand. He urged them to plead for mercy from the God of heaven concerning this mystery, so that he and his

friends might not be executed with the rest of Babylon's wise men. During the night, the mystery was revealed to Daniel in a vision. Then Daniel praised the God of heaven."[42]

4. **Problem-Solving**: Daniel not only interpreted the dream but also provided strategic advice to the king, showcasing his ability to apply his insights to real-world situations and offer practical solutions.

"I have found a man among the exiles from Judah who can tell the king the meaning of his dream.' The king said to Daniel (also called Belteshazzar), 'Are you able to tell me what I saw in my dream and what it means?' Daniel replied, 'None of the wise men, enchanters, magicians, or fortune-tellers can reveal the king's secret. But there is a God in heaven who reveals secrets, and he has shown King Nebuchadnezzar what will happen in the future.'"[43]

4. **Consistent Excellence**: Throughout his career, Daniel maintained consistent excellence and high standards, which earned him respect and distinction throughout his service.

"Soon Daniel was put in charge of the whole

government, second only to the king himself. He had such exceptional gifts that the king planned to put him in charge of the entire kingdom."[44]

2.3 Lessons for Modern Productivity:

1. **Ethical Foundation**: Daniel's steadfast adherence to his principles emphasises that productivity is most effective when grounded in strong ethical values. This aligns with modern concepts of "ethical leadership" and "values-based management"[45] For instance, if you're leading a team, making decisions that reflect honesty, integrity, and fairness will build trust and long-term success. Productivity is not at the expense of values and ethics. No doubt, prioritising ethical practices, will enhance its reputation and foster a loyal customer base.

2. **Continuous Learning and Adaptation**: Daniel's excellence in various fields of study reflects the emphasis on lifelong learning and adaptability. This connects to the theory of "growth mindset" developed by psychologist Carol Dweck, which posits that abilities and intelligence can be developed through dedication and hard work.[46] In practical terms, this could mean pursuing ongoing education, attending workshops, or staying updated with industry trends.

3. **Spiritual Intelligence**: "But there is a spirit in man: and the inspiration of the Almighty giveth them understanding."[47] Divine inspiration and the presence of God's spirit are crucial sources of wisdom and discernment. Daniel's life is a prime example of this. His reliance on God's wisdom not only helped him interpret dreams and solve complex problems but also guided his decision-making and actions.

> "But where can wisdom be found? Where does understanding dwell? No mortal comprehends its worth; it cannot be found in the land of the living. The deep says, "It is not in me"; the sea says, "It is not with me." It cannot be bought with the finest gold, nor can its price be weighed out in silver.
>
> The topaz of Cush cannot compare with it; it cannot be bought with pure gold. Where then does wisdom come from? Where does understanding dwell? It is hidden from the eyes of every living thing, conccaled even from the birds in the sky. God understands the way to it and he alone knows where it dwells, for he views the ends of the earth and sees everything under the heavens."[48]

4. **Cultural Intelligence**: Daniel's ability to thrive in a foreign culture while maintaining his identity demonstrates the importance of cultural intelligence in today's globalized world.[49] This involves understanding, respecting, and adapting to diverse cultures and perspectives. Context matters, don't forget that. For example, if you're working in a multinational team, being aware of and sensitive to different cultural practices can improve communication and collaboration.

Let's close our experience in this book with the Productivity Tree worksheet. I'm sure you'd find it very helpful. Here you go:

The Productivity Tree Worksheet

Crafting a Life of Purpose and Productivity: From Produce to Products

Welcome to the Productivity Tree Worksheet! This tool is designed to help you align your talents and abilities with your goals, transforming your raw potential into valuable outcomes. By understanding and refining your "produce" (innate talents and skills) and converting them into meaningful "products" (achievements and results), you can cultivate a life of purpose and productivity.

Part 1: Identifying Your "Produce"

1. Reflect on and list your raw talents, gifts, and abilities. These are the foundational elements of your "produce. *(See your previous Potent-Intent Worksheet)*

_____

_____

_____

2. For "produce," describe how it currently manifests in your life or work. This will help you understand how these raw elements are currently being utilized.

Part 2: From Produce to Products

1. For each "produce" item, think about the potential "products" (valuable outputs):

For each item listed in Part 1, iterate potential "products"—valuable outputs or results that you can achieve by leveraging these talents.

Produce	Potential Products

2. Which of these products align best with your professional goals and life's purpose?

3. What steps can you take to refine your "produce" into these "products"?

Part 3: Assessing Your Production Process

1. List your current main activities in a typical work week:

Activities	Time/Man-hours

2. For each activity, evaluate:

Is this activity transforming my "produce" into valuable "products"? (Yes/No). If yes, how can I enhance this process? If no, how can I modify or replace this activity?

Activities	Remarks

Part 4: Your Productivity Tree

Visualize your productivity as a tree, with your "produce" as the roots, your activities as the trunk and branches, and your "products" as the fruits.

1. Sketch your current "productivity tree". Label the roots, trunk, branches, and fruits.

2. Now, sketch your ideal "productivity tree" for one year from now. What has changed?

3. What specific steps will you take to nurture your tree from its current state to your ideal state?

Note: True productivity isn't about being busy; it's about making meaningful progress towards your goals and purpose. Nurture your "Productivity Tree" with intention, and watch it bear fruit in due season!

Highest Learning Points

Take a moment to jot down and highlight the key insights and lessons that resonated with you most in this chapter.

Abraham O. Owoseni

Most Pressing Action Points

Take a moment to note down the key decisions and actions you would take based on the insights gained from this chapter.

END NOTES

[1] Genesis 1:28 MSG
[2] Drucker, P. F. (2006). The effective executive: The definitive guide to getting the right things done. HarperBusiness.
[3] Covey, S. R. (1989). The 7 habits of highly effective people: Powerful lessons in personal change. Free Press.
[4] Newport, C. (2016). Deep work: Rules for focused success in a distracted world. Grand Central Publishing.
[5] Drucker, P. F., & Maciariello, J. A. (2008). The Drucker Lectures: Essential Lessons on Management, Society, and Economy. McGraw-Hill Education.
[6, 7] Matthew 25:29 ICB, TLB
[8] Genesis 1:11-12 NIV
[9] Genesis 1:28 MSG
[10] Psalm 1.3 AMP
[11] 2 Kings 4:1-7 AMP
[12] Hidalgo, C. A., & Hausmann, R. (2009). The building blocks of economic complexity. Proceedings of the National Academy of Sciences, 106(26), 10570-10575.
[13] Cunningham S. (2017). Economic complexity, the Product Space and structural change.
[14] Genesis 1:2 NET
[15] Genesis 1:2b
[16] Job 32.8
[17] John 6: 5-6 MSG
[18] John 6: 7 ICB
[19] John 6: 8-9 ICB
[20] John 6: 10-13 ICB
[21] Genesis 1:3 NLT
[22] Hebrews 11:3 NKJV
[23] Matthew 25:24-28
[24] Genesis 41:16

[25] 1 Corinthians 4:7 ICB
[26] James 4:6 TPT
[27] Genesis 37:3-4 MSG
[28] Genesis 41:33-36
[29] Genesis 41:57
[30] Genesis 41:25-32 TPT
[31] Genesis 41:30-31 AMPC
[32] Genesis 41:33-36 TLB
[33] Genesis 41:37-40 TLB
[34] Genesis 41:56-57 NIV
[35] Rohrbeck, R., Battistella, C., & Huizingh, E. (2015). Corporate foresight: An emerging field with a rich tradition. *Technological Forecasting and Social Change*, 101, 1-9.
[36] Senge, P. M. (2006). The fifth discipline: The art and practice of the learning organization. Second edition. Random House
[40] Daniel 1:8-16 NLT
[41] Daniel 1:17-20 AMPC
[42] Daniel 2:17-19 TPT
[43] Daniel 2:24-45 NLT
[44] Daniel 6:3 MSG
[45] Brown, M. E., & Treviño, L. K. (2006). Ethical leadership: A review and future directions. The Leadership Quarterly, 17(6), 595-616.
[46] Dweck, C. S. (2006). Mindset: The new psychology of success. Random House
[47] Job 32:8 KJV
[48] Job 28: 12-16, 19-21, 23-24 TLB
[49] Earley, P. C., & Ang, S. (2003). Cultural intelligence: Individual interactions across cultures. Stanford University Press.

Scripture quotations used in this book are from the following translations: ICB (International Children's Bible): © *1986, 1988, 1999, 2015 by Thomas Nelson, Inc. BBE (Bible in Basic English): Public Domain* © *1965 by Cambridge University Press. CEV (Contemporary English Version):* © *1991, 1992, 1995 by American Bible Society. NIV (New International Version):* © *1973, 1978, 1984, 2011 by Biblica, Inc.*™ *AMPC (Amplified Bible, Classic Edition):* © *1954, 1958, 1962, 1964, 1965, 1987 by The Lockman Foundation. AMP (Amplified Bible):* © *2015 by The Lockman Foundation. GW (God's Word Translation):* © *1995 by God's Word to the Nations. Used by permission of Baker Publishing Group. TPT (The Passion Translation):* © *2017, 2018 by BroadStreet Publishing Group, LLC. NLT (New Living Translation):* © *1996, 2004, 2007, 2015 by Tyndale House Foundation. TLB (The Living Bible):* © *1971, 1986 by permission of Tyndale House Publishers, Inc. KJV (King James Version). MSG (The Message):* © *1993, 1994, 1995, 1996, 2000, 2001, 2002 by Eugene H. Peterson. NKJV (New King James Version):* © *1982 by Thomas Nelson, Inc. NASB (New American Standard Bible):* © *1960, 1962, 1963, 1968, 1971, 1972, 1973, 1975, 1977, 1995 by The Lockman Foundation. EASY (EasyEnglish Bible:* © *MissionAssist 2019 - Charitable Incorporated Organisation 1162807. Used by permission.*

AS A BONUS,

access your free resource

at www.abrahamowoseni.com

TRANSFORMED LIVES
Featured Testimonials

I have known Dr. Abraham since 2022 and have appreciated his gifts from afar ever since. Even though he doesn't know me, he inspires me. It was a privilege to listen to him teach "The Power of Potential" for the second time; the experience was fresh and re-inspiring.

I was at the edge of my chair during the class and could not take my eyes off the screen nor could I break from writing. The quotes were truly insightful; I had to write them all down. Dr. Abraham's identification of the potentials in Bible characters, how he mimicked what they must have said to themselves to recognize their gifts, and how they utilized them, stood out for me.

Additionally, the stories he shared to explain how God expressed His power through the gifts He has given us were impactful. I realized I could apply the identification process used by those characters. Now, my new mindset is that I should convert my potential into a skill version to make it easily presentable and accessible to the world. My experience with Dr. Abraham Owoseni was very insightful.

—Sajo O.

I am so grateful that I met with Dr. Abraham. He has been such a blessing even though I have never met him face to face. Truly, I believe that it was God who directed Dr. Abraham to me at this point in my life. From the Clarity Coaching Speed Call, he gave me a very good understanding of what I should do and my purpose. I had low self-esteem and was not too sure of what to do with my life. I was never the top student;

I was average, never really knowing what to do next.

I actually thought that the course was going to be a normal course or teaching on how to overcome bad habits, but it was different and way more than that. I loved this course because it changed my perspective of things—how I should do things, what I should say, and what is needed to be let go of. It gave me a big sense of responsibility. Truly, his teaching has made me think far better than I did in the past, and I cannot truly use words to describe how grateful I am.

He really is God-sent, and I am grateful to God that I am part of the people that God sent him to. It has been mind-transforming in every area. I love it and I pray that God keeps blessing Dr. Abraham with more grace to reach out to more young people and youths.

—Oghenemaro E.

My experience with Dr. Abraham was wonderful, inspiring, and educational. I had known Dr. Abraham for a long time, but he came at the right time to help build and prepare me spiritually and physically for the future. What has changed in my mindset is my approach to building relationships. I have learned to be more receptive and I've become more accommodating, but without compromising godly virtues and moral values in place of friendship.

I particularly enjoyed Chapter 3 of the book, "*Camp Us.*" What stood out to me was the concept of adding '*SPICE*' to grow in maturity, just as spice is essential in food.

—Oluwatomiwa O.

I was on the verge of giving up on my academics, but his charismatic and enthusiastic teaching on overcoming obstacles to academic breakthrough ignited the spirit of excellence and diligence within me.

His teachings at the second-day workshop for academic breakthrough at the Annual Youth Alive Convention AYAC 2024 were profoundly impactful. He is very motivational, experienced and his teachings are transformational. Also the spirit of excellence in him is contagious. My experience with Dr. Abraham Owoseni was both motivational and transformational.

—Toluwanimi

My experience with Dr. Abraham Owoseni was exceptional throughout the second semester of my first year Master's program. Almost every class moment was highly appealing to me. Dr. Owoseni's lectures made me develop a deeper passion for the course. His life experiences and lessons shared in class were memorable and extended beyond the typical classroom setting. The class presentations and discussions made the course more interesting and engaging, showcasing his quick thinking and intelligence both as a lecturer and as a person.

During this time, my mind and skillset have grown significantly. Dr. Owoseni has greatly enhanced my diversity in learning and thinking, as well as my engagement and presentation skills. I have gained valuable insights from his knowledge and experience, as well as from his motivational talks. Dr. Abraham Owoseni is truly a man of value. Thank you, sir, for being wonderful.

—Oluwadamilola O.

This session is one I would define as electrifying; it's one of those experiences that sets fire in your bones. I love how practical Dr. Abraham's approach to learning is, how he made reference to the Bible in such a lively way with insights and spiritual understanding. It re-awakened passion in me to live a purposeful and value-adding life. More than ever now, I know that I can't afford to run this race called life without knowing God's purpose for my life. I think this will be the first time I am seeing the truth that God does not delight in my confusion, but desires that I understand His purpose for which He created me, because everything starts with the purpose why He created me.

—Heritage K.

"Inspirational" is always the word, I think Dr. Abraham's ability to see things through other people's lens makes his answers just on point, accurate and inspiring. Many instances mentioned were very relatable and in all very insightful! I'm now working on strategic answers prepared beforehand for vital common questions as taught during the presentation. I've also had to rethink the reason why I'm doing what I'm doing to put it in the right perspective.

—Demilade O.

I actually meant to send this a while ago. I attended the Revolution Summit you facilitated in July 2022. It was a deeply insightful experience for me. It changed my perspective on the meaning of success. I understood that true success would require balance across all areas of life and would ultimately result in the growth of a person. Discovery leads to revolution and revolution must lead to evolution. I also read the Maturity Handbook. I am quite confident that with the concepts you discussed at that event, and the many more I uncover while perpetually learning through life, I am on track to lead a life of good balance. I am grateful to you and your team for putting these together for us and I have no doubts that great rewards are in line for you. God bless you richly Sir. Cheers.

—Isaac I.

Read more at https://abrahamowoseni.com/testimonials/

USEFUL RESOURCES

What an incredible journey it has been! I hope you found this experience valuable. Here are some other recommended books and transformational learning resources by Dr. Abraham Owoseni

Explore and Order Other Impactful Books by Dr. Abraham Owoseni:

[Category] Clarity, Career and Leadership

The Career Dashboard: Eight (8) Vital Indicators to Monitor & Thrive in Your Career.

Success Redefined: The Inside-Out Approach. (Achieving All-Round Success Regardless of Background, Circumstances, or Limitations)

Lead-a-Ship: Navigating Success in Managerial Positions

E-Motions: How to Work with the Head and the Hand Without Losing the Heart

Living by Design: Go Beyond Existing to Truly Live out God's Purpose for Your Life

The Next Chapter: How to Navigate the Next Season of Life With Clarity and Confidence

The Career Leader: A Guide to Purposeful Career and Influential Leadership

[Category] Relationships and Lifestyle

The Wait is Over: How Mums and Dads can Trust God to Receive their Godly Seeds by Sarah O. Owoseni

Starting a New Home: A Young Adult's Guide to a Well-balanced Family Life

Values of a Father: Fatherhood-Parenting and Nation Building

Fellows-in-a-Ship: How to Start the Friendship that Leads to Courtship Without Shipwreck

The In-Betweens: How to Navigate Relationships Beyond the Ecstasy of Rings, Flowers and Perfect Pictures

The Maturity Handbook: 30 Days of Deep Reflections, Uncommon Wisdom, and All-round Development

The Architecture of Goals: How to Design, Develop and Live Out Your Goals Seamlessly

Goal Setting Quickie: A Quick Fix to Getting Better Results & Setting Higher-Order Goals

[Category] Academics and Personal Development

Camp Us: A Memoir for a Smooth Academic Sail in the Higher Institution

Life During & After School: How to Make Schooling Fun & Exciting Without Painful Memories & Future Regrets

Explore and order at abrahamowoseni.com/resources

Online Courses

Online Course on Purpose discovery & Clarity:

Enroll at **abrahamowoseni.com**

> **Finding Clarity, Purpose and Meaning:** Discover your Life's Purpose, Unlock Your Best Life and Position for All-round Success on Auto-pilot

Online Courses on Career Harmony and Development:

Enroll at **abrahamowoseni.com**

> **Career Starter Pack**
>
> [Revealed] Untold Secrets to Starting & Growing a Purposeful, Profitable & Promising Career Journey
>
> **Career Growth Accelerator:** Increasing your Earning Capacity and Fast Tracking Your Career
>
> **Public Speaking Secrets:** How to Advance your Reputation and Influence through High-Performing Presentations as a Career Leader

Online Courses on Lifestyle Harmony and Development: Enroll at **abrahamowoseni.com**

> **Personal Mastery:** Unconventional Strategies for Effective Self-Management and Emotional Healing

Habit Mastery & Confidence Upgrade: Stop Any Unwanted Habit, Sustain Productive Ones and Turbo-charge your Self-worth

Workplace Success Kit

Core Skills to Elevate your Attitude, Charisma, and Lifestyle.

Online Courses on Relationship Harmony and Development:

Friendship, Not Dating: Redefining Relationships and Building Genuine Friendship and People Skills

Before the Ring: Getting your Conviction Right in Choosing a Life Partner and Maximising the Courtship Season

Beyond the Ring: Strengthening Your Marriage Beyond the Wedding Day, Preparing to Conceive and Nurturing Godly Children

ACKNOWLEDGEMENTS

I extend my heartfelt gratitude to everyone who has contributed to the creation of Produce and Prosper. Your unwavering support and contribution have been instrumental throughout this journey.

I'm grateful to God for the divine inspiration, strength, and wisdom that guided me in birthing this message for the world.

I would like to express my gratitude to my mentors and spiritual leaders who have laid a strong foundation for my understanding of productivity and purpose. A special thank you to Mr. Remi Dairo for your invaluable coaching and for graciously writing the foreword to this book.

To my students, clients, course takers and participants at my workshops, events and seminars—your enthusiasm and commitment to growth inspired me to share these principles more broadly. Thank you for being a source of motivation.

I am also grateful to my family for their endless love and support. To my beloved wife and children, your gift has been the bedrock of my journey, providing me with the harmony to live full and fulfilling.

Finally, I hope this book serves as a catalyst for your transformation, empowering you to embrace your God-given purpose and redefine your understanding of productivity. I can't wait to hear your impact story. Go for it!

ABOUT THE AUTHOR
Abraham O. Owoseni, Ph.D.

Dr. Abraham Owoseni is a transformational leader impacting lives through ministry, education, and human development. His three-part mission transforms how we live, work, and learn using an integrated approach that addresses the holistic needs of individuals. His teachings on life skills and his message of all-round success and holistic development have been instrumental in moulding minds and raising kingdom-driven, wholesome leaders.

Dr. Abraham teaches God's Word with simplicity and clarity, emphasising practical application in everyday living. His corporate training sessions, online courses, masterclasses and life and career coaching programs have helped numerous individuals build purposeful careers, enhance productivity, and lead wholesome lives. A first-class graduate from Covenant University, Dr. Abraham holds a PhD focused on improving learning environments with multiple certifications across various domains.

With a direct impact on thousands of lives, he has delivered hundreds of keynote speeches and structured presentations, appeared on numerous radio and TV interviews, and authored several books and knowledge products. His multidisciplinary expertise is sought after by a wide range of organizations, from non-profits and educational institutions to corporations and faith-based institutions.

For more information about Dr. Abraham's work and global impact, please visit abrahamowoseni.com

Connect with Dr. Abraham Owoseni:

Email:	ab@abrahamowoseni.com
Instagram:	@abrahamowoseni
LinkedIn:	@abrahamowoseni
Facebook:	@LifeSkillsExpert
Twitter/X:	@AbrahamOwoseni
YouTube:	@AbrahamOwoseni

www.ingramcontent.com/pod-product-compliance
Lightning Source LLC
Chambersburg PA
CBHW052303220526
45471CB00001B/466